PERU: THE NEW POETRY

PERU

The New Poetry

Edited by
MAUREEN AHERN and DAVID TIPTON

LONDON MAGAZINE EDITIONS 1970

NOTE

All the translations in this book are by us, jointly, except where otherwise stated in the text.

Acknowledgements are due to the editors of the following magazines in which some of these translations first appeared: *Grosseteste Review*, *Haravec* (Peru), *Iconolatre*, *London Magazine*, *Stand*, *Tri-Quarterly* and *Twentieth Century*. Acknowledgements and gratitude are also due to the authors and publishers of the original Spanish texts for permission to translate.

Our appreciation and gratitude to the following people to whom we are indebted for their help: ENA HOLLIS for the translations of the poems indicated in the text; to WILLIAM ROWE for advice and assistance with the translations of Antonio Cisneros; to MIRKO LAUER for help with his own poems; ALITA LOMELLINI for her assistance in the following translations: *Testament*, *Shades of Origin* and *Interior Patio* by Salazar Bondy; *Our House* and *Quijote* by Marco Martos; to RICHARD GREENWELL for assistance in the translations of Gonzalo Rose.

M. A.
D. T.

30 Thurloe Place, S.W.7

SBN 900626 16 X

Printed in Great Britain by
Billing & Sons Ltd., Guildford and London

CONTENTS

INTRODUCTION

Peru, inward-looking, seeking its identity as a nation, with a military government simultaneously revolutionary and chauvinistic, is a country in a state of turmoil. Its sense of having been exploited, and of social injustice, has led to the take-over of foreign companies and to Agrarian Reform, both inevitable steps, but also to extremes of nationalism. Yesterday I watched a troop of short dark-skinned soldiers in their red and blue uniforms—the officer's covered in gold braid—with drawn swords and to the accompaniment of a band, take down the flag flying above a site that commemorates some 19th-century battle against Chile. It was dusk, the ceremony watched by a solemn and enthusiastic crowd. It was symptomatic. As was the response recently to Peru's victory over Argentina and Bolivia in the *World Cup*, when cavalcades of cars honked through the streets and a mass hysteria was released: the football victory providing a common ground of identity. Neither the Cuban Revolution nor the death of Ché Guevara has been so significant over the last few years as this sense of emerging from a state of under-development into the mid-twentieth century. And the poetry of the 'sixties reflects, and comes from the same turmoil and confusion, tension and vitality.

Modern Peruvian poetry is generally considered to have been dominated by three figures: José María Eguren, César Vallejo and Martín Adán. Of the three by far the most important is Vallejo, whose work is rooted in the landscape and social structure of his environment. Born in an Andean town still medieval in outlook, from a deeply religious family, becoming Marxist, he produced a confessional and dramatic poetry that could only have come from the uniqueness of his background and life. Whereas Eguren wrote a 'pure' or 'essentialist' poetry much influenced by European writing, and having little connection with the actuality of Peru. Martín Adán, still alive and writing, suffers from periodic bouts of mental illness, and has published little in the last decade. In 1960, when he was in Peru, Allen Ginsberg met Adán in one of the little bars in the old section of Lima. They became friendly, and Ginsberg persuaded him to collect a batch of poems written on tattered bits of paper for a new book. They turned out to be formal sonnets, 'pure and clean', whereas Ginsberg had hoped for his 'dirtiest secret scribblings'. (*To an old poet in Peru*, from *Reality Sandwiches*, City Lights, 1964).

Surrealism had considerable impact upon writers in the 'thirties and 'forties, such as Westphalen, Eilson and Blanca Varela, who came from cultured backgrounds, their influences tending to be European, their interests abstract and philosophical. Other poets of that period, the *Indigenistas*, searching for roots in the songs and legends of the Quechua, extolled Inca and Indian traditions. The best of these is Alejandro Peralta, but much of their work seems artificial and self-conscious. José María Argüedas in his novels more effectively reveals the spirit of the Indian and his life in the sierra. He knew it intimately and spoke Quechua before he learnt Spanish.

By the 'fifties, however, two schools predominated: the *Social-realists* using their poetry as a direct weapon in the service of Marxism, and to denounce the harsh social system, though the most prominent, Romualdo, Rose and Delgado, have since moved away from the sterility demanded by such narrow concepts and are producing a more subjective poetry; and the *Purists*, seeking a verbal and stylistic perfection, who wrote of the 'interior life' intending 'revelation through the word', their poetry claiming to be 'a song to beauty'. The best among the *Purists* is Sologuren who deserves special mention, for more than anyone else he has fostered new poets, publishing their first books from his handpress, *La Rama Florida*, and encouraging them with advice.

Though traces of all these influences can be seen in the work of the poets here, there's also something distinctive and peculiar to the 'sixties, and it is in the work of Carlos Germán Belli (*O Hada Cibernética*, 1961), and Pablo Guevara (*Los Habitantes*, 1965), that we see the beginnings of this. Of the two, Guevara, experimental and influenced by poets such as Ezra Pound, has had the most direct influence upon the younger group of poets in this anthology.

Poets tend to develop early here, to publish their first books and establish reputations while young, then often fail to fulfil their initial promise. 'The writer in our countries has had to split himself, separate his vocation from his daily activity, multiply himself in a thousand jobs that deprived him of the time necessary for writing; jobs that often revolted his conscience and convictions . . . Our societies have encouraged a constant mistrust towards this marginal creature, who against all reason has set himself to practice an art that in the Latin American circumstances is virtually unreal. This is why our writers have failed by the dozen, deserted their vocation or betrayed it by practising it in a half-hearted and hidden fashion without diligence or discipline.' (Vargas Llosa, *Fate and Mission of the Writer in Latin America*, 1967.)

A year before Vallejo's death in 1937, a brilliantly promising young Peruvian, Oquendo de Amat, died in the charity ward of a

Madrid hospital. He had published one book, *5 metres of poetry*, 1927. In 1931 he left for Europe, was dragged from his boat in Central America, no one knows why, imprisoned, interrogated and tortured, thus arriving in Spain broken in health. Javier Heraud, after two years studying in Cuba, re-entered Peru illegally and took up arms as a guerrilla. He was shot by police as he floated in a canoe down the Madre de Dios River in the wildest and most remote region of the eastern jungle. He had put the ideals of many into practice and died for them. To others his seemed a brave but futile gesture exemplifying their dilemma.

These are extreme cases, but inevitably the social and economic problems of Peru deeply affect the writer, driving many into exile and others into abandoning their work. 'The Latin-American situation offers a virtual orgy of motives for being a rebel and living dissatisfied' (Vargas Llosa). Social conditions are changing, as change they must, but far too slowly for the majority of intellectuals who, coming from the middle class and usually settling in Lima, are unable to come to terms with their situation. Some remain as teachers, professors or journalists, but others unwilling to risk compromising their talents, live abroad. Yet despite this, or perhaps out of this situation, over the last decade, poetry has emerged owing little to the prevailing modes of the 'forties and 'fifties, and which some believe to be the best since Vallejo, and among the most exciting in Latin-America today.

DAVID TIPTON
Lima, November 1969

Sebastian Salazar Bondy

Testament

I'll leave my shadow
a sharp needle that wounds the street,
with sad eyes examines the walls,
the latticed windows of impotent loves
& the shrouded sky of Lima.
I'll leave my ghostly fingers
that touched the keys, bellies, water, eyelids of honey
& from which the writing came
like a virgin with an untrammelled soul.
I'll leave my egg-shaped skull, my spiders' feet
my suit burnt by the ash of omens
& discoloured by the fire of nocturnal books.
I'll leave my fluttering wings, my typewriter
that galloped like a small horse year after year
in search of the essence where death dies.
I'll leave several notebooks worm-eaten by sloth
a few wilful images of the world
between flashes & tears
like dust in the teeth.
Take them, gather them in your skirt like crumbs
& feed oblivion with such delicacies.

Translated by David Tipton

Shades of Origin

I was born in a flimsy nest
of adobe & cane from Guayaquil,
on a street named, *Corazón de Jesús*, where now
a mechanic's yard is going broke,
where no one talked of Communism
except in secret in some workers' families
& the word sounded distant,
dragging itself between walls of fog &
through long winter silences.
A flimsy nest hidden
among the damp branches of Lima
with mutilated birds against the sky,
a reckless challenge, it's true.
Around the nest rusty patience,
narrow patios, corners of forbidden beauty,
clocks in shadow,
alcoves like wharfs & the stares of madmen,
yet despite this my small world seemed infinite;
the poor found ecstasy in saints' processions,
the pale drizzle of the priests
& the esoteric ritual of extreme unction;
& old father Sunday
dressed the neighbourhood with his ragged dances.
And at times staccato human shouts
hawked fruit & honey, grindstones & *tamales*,
& scared of the flu epidemics
neighbours called the vendors

to their shuttered windows.
In the distance the sea breathed
its chemical monotony of iodised air,
slow livid waters
without direction or dangers.
I was either tears or laughter
everything in opposites,
soft
tough
dark
sunny.
I always came back to that leafy room,
the bobbin of adobe & cane,
the suspended pit in the shadows of origin
with its unrepeatable union of smells & warmth.
I was born in a flimsy nest
& its possible loss
oppressed my childhood dreams with terror.

Translated by David Tipton

Without Knowing Why

One morning of ancestral ash
I discovered the roads to the desert,
farewells like a mirage sparkling in the sand.
The nest was crooked in the branches
its flimsy door of love condemned
by its rough & dumb adobe.
Nobody knew why man had nurtured war
nor why he'd put hyenas & barbed-wire

facing the west, musical & sacred like wheat,
nor why bats regular as newspapers
covered the countryside with their wings; we saw
Indians like noble stones cracked by the centuries,
Heads of State comfortably settled behind their election figures,
& arid markets of yarn
languid alleys full of prejudiced believers,
cars with whores & their docile admirers,
broken things
distant provinces
plush residences
& the bureaucratic gods sweating in their offices,
consumptive, perverse gentlemen
surrounded by wars, hyenas, newspapers & unnecessary statistics.
What can be done?
Where can we look
except on someone caged?
What's there to contemplate
if the mirror is stormy
& in it no narcissus to adore his youth?
What degree to opt for?
What commemorative plaque to unveil?
What baroque belfries to ponder over
like Spanish-American jewels?
The scorching question
filled the morning with its ash
—for what,
why did they discover this last savage land?

Translated by Ena Hollis & David Tipton

Exiled from the Light

The President caressed the mane of his favourite horse.
The white icy hand
the same that signed decrees of tyranny,
that gestured in the Te Deum his faithless prayers
& fondled the bodies of maids
as he put on their checkered uniforms,
the same
            hard hand
                        of the President.
A pallid hand that sold human flesh
that with its userer's rings
blessed the downtrodden race
& flushed sensually when he died.
At that time people flowed through the streets,
a slow river that clogged the corners,
drifted to the taverns
fell in with the fetid torrent of the procession
& the bullfight,
& in the leaden afternoon
returning to the suburbs,
whirled like a number in the wheel of misfortune.
Men rubbing out their identities with alcohol,
cursing the pregnant bellies of their homes,
called under their breath
to that anonymous free man
                                who in the end
would deal vengeance to this false god.

And that's how it happened.
A major slashed on the block
that leonine & capricious mane,
but he was another lion,
who restored fear to the marriage beds,
oppressed the ignorant & isolated the poor
with a black shirt of violence.
So the trigger-finger was forged
from the ember of that first murder
& when he rode triumphantly before the crowds,
behind the cheers, a gunshot cut him down,
another
            & another
returning his wolf's glory to the executioner.
The table was like a last supper,
a poem of roses & geometry,
a guitar evoking sad tears,
& someone coughed between the grating,
someone that scrabbled in the swamp
& disappeared,
a flutter of doves sacrificed in the dark,
the sun toppled from its easy throne—
for everyone
                    you have to say that
                                        but not for us,
poor Peruvians exiled from the light.

Translated by Ena Hollis & Maureen Ahern

Interio Patio

Old tenacious boards
that've seen so many families leave,
turn to dust & drizzle
& return like a wave to the dunes,
I owe you something,
money, melancholy, sadness,
a certain cloistered silver ash.

Rotting columns that still
support drawing-rooms, bedrooms, the pantry
& the kitchen that smokes with some frugal smell,
I owe you riches without anger
& long thoughtful pallor.

Interior patio,
crow of lazy mists,
between whose feathers lovers
dissolved like an inscription
on a handkerchief,
I owe you this moment,
my glowing vice,
I inhabit you & scold you
& sign my name upon you with a knife.

Translated by David Tipton

Francisco Carrillo

I Love my Country

I love my country,
its myths & legends,
its tin symbols
& other lies.

I love my country
& I'd like to shout it out
like any chauvinist
because though I'm not entirely honest
I'm Peruvian too,
the kind that gets sad
when he hears the national anthem;
& after a military parade for Independence Day
just like any idiot
I'd like to get excited with ten *soles*
& cheer for Peru & its President.

I love my country
& I'd like to love its Indians too
—the concrete symbols—
its petroleum & foreign mines,
its coarse slave-driving politicians
its pedagogic & chimerical history.

Peruvian that I am, or because I am,
I've betrayed it too
& the only thing I'm left with

is the privilege of being
at sometime
its prodigal son.

The Tannery

A swarm of flies is drumming on
some blackened hide, ragged & infected,
while the sun excitedly woos
the black-green water in the vat.

An Indian washes his mouldy feet
in the putrid ashen water
& with the cocaine settled in his brain
his patience pulses impotently.

In their tilted hats the women
poke the maize & wail a *huayno.*
In a vague stupor of excrement
the children wallow with the pigs.

Tomorrow the conman, an agent from the coast,
will exploit their work for peanuts
& on Sunday he'll further sap their energy
with the sluggish *chicha* of the church.

Procession

A ragged block of rockets breaks up
the evening with its colour
& drives the herd into the dung-spread entrance
with the martial rhythm of a *pasodoble.*

A corpulent priest behind the incense
slyly ferrets out some new conquest
& protected by his cassock intones a prayer
to his humiliated Christ.

(The mountain girls, lined up & penitent,
chant in the totality of their ignorance.)

Later on, blessed by lechery,
with the sunset spilt across the hills,
they'll run into concrete eternity
in the humble sincerity of a craftsman.

Composition 1

It's raining,
it rains in Lima with a frivolous drizzle.

Small drops pearl the jackets
of morose office workers.

It must be sad to be poor
in this tuberculer & useless rain.
Today I feel like stopping at some corner
to have a coffee & warm my soul;
meet a friend, sit down & smoke
& not to talk at all.

Today I'd like to flirt with some working-girl.

Yet, the beautiful girls like
            walking in this rain.
(I remember once, in a place where
            it really used to rain,
I sinned in my bedroom
& the rain around me smiled.)

Many poets are inspired
& suffer in the rain.
It used to oppress Vallejo, for example . . .
& there's a beautiful poem about the rain.

But I—a pallid citizen—live in Chosica,
have a car
& eat well everyday.
And this talking of the rain that redeems others
smacks of fantasy to me,
of an artificial sadness in shop windows,
a brief combination of inertia
& my own uncertain poetical convictions.

Provincia

1

Six o'clock. The cathedral blesses
the belltower's morning hymn
& the shadow of religious women sidles
along the candid mission of its rosary.

A lover hurriedly squeezes through
the gate that leads into a garden
& a peasant who has slept in the street
begins to chant his final *huayno.*

Six o'clock. The reddened
Andean sun drags in the morning
& the surrounding country bristles
with hopes that move towards the market.

2

After an exceptional day of work
with the sunset fresh monotonous gossip
that day by day regulates
the tragic prison of the province.

Shy spinsters in the park
display their modest hopes.
The dusty country stretches out
beyond the colonial suburbs.

And there're sunny days to bore you
drinking away the lazy afternoons
or watching the procession that slowly
becomes the highlight of the week.

Only some orgy begun with literary intentions
or the alcoholic scandal of some priest
at a humble wake in the vicinity
save you from total softening of the brain.

All Souls' Day

The colonial cemetery wears
its poncho of festive colours
& evokes from a 100 miles around
memories of the last Imperial fiestas.

Sober Indians around the mourners
mutter thoughtful gibberish
while their kids trample between the crosses
which they'll later pee upon.

Traditional priests comfortably fill
their greasy bishops' cassocks,
for the stipend mumble tepid hopes
in stuttered paternosters.

People listen to the bloody awful Latin
& the burial corners 're sweetened by their responses.
A drunken believer's getting maudlin
because he wants to fulfil his charges.

In the evening *charango* bands strike up
there's fly-covered spicy food & brandy
& with the night the final violence
is passified by tearful sex.

Washington Delgado

Imperfect Times

Peru was a chimera,
gold, dust, sabres,
orphanhood,
hunger, penury, death.

Tomorrow,
what will it be?

History of Peru

There's no past
only a multitude
of dead.
There are no Incas,
Viceroys
or Great-Captains,
only a hundred
yellow papers
& a little land.
There was a landowner
who said to his slaves:
Gold is good
& God is in Heaven.
There was a soldier
who said to those
that listened:

I kill because they pay me
& I know nothing of Heaven.
But this not a history
only twenty words
that say nothing.

Translated by David Tipton

Human Wisdom

When someone talks of the spirit
look out for your pocket.
This is the wisdom that came to us
from a place called the West.

Before this the sun shone
above, below & inside.
This belief gave strength
to arms & passion to the mouth.

A man had a house,
a function, a soul,
a position & a worth
among men.

Later came the other people
who had courage
& weighed gold.
They taught us.

Now we live with prisons,
bishops & soldiers. Now we know

that one thing is good
& another bad.

And that pain isn't pain
nor is hunger hunger
& that in some part of Heaven
we're all equal.

Translated by David Tipton

Good Manners

It's dangerous to walk
with a name on your lips.
Never say
Spain, Leningrad, girl,
dear land.
Learn the good manners of life,
life is silent
& silence has many words:
good morning, summer's come,
prices'll rise
if salaries rise, the land awaits
your sacrifice, the president
deplores the incident, the ministers
trust in the future, the murderer
was judged
& God blesses our people.
Old sweet words
useless & tender
as dated almanacks.

So why say
Spain, Leningrad, girl,
dear land?
Don't walk around
with a name on your lips.

Translated by David Tipton

Life Explains & Death Spies Out

Reality gathers
my papers, arranges the furniture
in my house, skilfully
piles up in the plazas,
floats on the sea, proclaims
its aroma in the market.
In my dreams it builds
pyramids & letters.

Reality enfolds me
& is full
of sweet air & newspapers,
wherever I go I read it
& breathe it. Confuse
its size
& stumble into it
or it suddenly shifts
& stumbles into me.
In one way or another
it gags in my throat.

Reality
is within me.
I judge, pre-judge, ascertain
& make mistakes:
an implacable reality
governs me.

In bed I breathe; within me
reality breathes.
Some day or some night
I'll no longer breathe
& reality will have gone
from my house, my bed, my body
& from my soul.

Plurality of Worlds

Fifty worlds lie on my table,
parade around my room, turn on
the taps, look at me, call me
& divide among themselves each crumb of my body.
Fifty men live in my name,
read the letters of my dead mother,
listen in the newspapers
to the beat of a meaningless
history,
caress the yellow sands of Ancón
near the garbage dumps of history
or drink water & breathe air
infinitely transmuted
by mouths, noses, lungs,

hairs & roots immemorial.
At this time of day
the banana leaves shade me,
a fly buzzes & a small cloud
neither moves nor sounds.
I read Marx & know
that history repeats itself
& is a farce
that makes one weep.
I cherish certain expressions
in the faces of my children
who will die
in the middle of new garbage dumps.
At the cinema I see the story of Ivan
encircled by thick walls of stone,
crouched before the narrow gates,
smothered by eyes & words
& saved from the dagger & poison
because history is a farce
often repeated.
My books lie in piles
at the foot of my bed, on top
of the chair & on the table
where as I recall
it's time to eat.
The words of Horace & the small house
will never suffice me.
I'll not stand up against the sea's thrust,
nor will I slip on the winds,
I won't stay in my house.
I'll live once again
the beautiful words
that once again deceive me,

a gust of frustrated desires
or a game of love.
I sign the papers that prolong
the perhaps, in other words, necessity
or sadness.
In the jungle men
fight & die;
I light a cigarette & divide it among fifty
meaningless worlds.

Carlos Germán Belli

Segregation

My mother, my two brothers, myself
& many little Peruvians
dig a deep hole, deep down
where we hide,
because on top everything's owned,
everything's locked up,
sealed tight,
because on top everything's taken:
the tree's shade, flowers,
fruit, a roof, wheels,
water, pencils,
so we prefer to sink down
to the bottom of the earth,
deeper than ever,
far away from the bosses,
today, Sunday,
far far away from the owners,
among the feet of small creatures,
because up on top,
there's a few who run everything,
who write, sing, dance, &
speak beautifully,
& red with shame,
we want only to disintegrate
into small pieces.

Translated by Maureen Ahern

10 poems from
'O Hada Cibernética'

I

Why have they moved me
from womb
to earth
instead of spawning me
in water   air   or fire?

2

Fine that so much heaven for so many
is so much hell for me,
so I stand   & with each step
tearing away the chaff
strip off my skin   my bones
even my marrow.

4

Some day I'll finally
attain love
as it is among my dead betters:
not within their eyes, but without,
invisible & perennial,
if not of fire, of air.

5

I find myself—shinbones,
skin & gullet loitering
in this valley of infinite crap;
yet I'm sick of my contentment
for I have fewer bonds, less weight
& fewer days ahead.

7

Cold fear because looking at you
I see you more aloof than
yesterday you were angry
& it turns every pore of my body
into a stalking eye;
but must it always be so,
this skin bristling
with a thousand transfigured eyes.

9

An unknown voice told me:
'if they pull you out with forceps
from my luminous cloister, foetus,
you'll never lie with Phylis in the meadow;'
& now after three decades,
finding myself in this sullen lodging,
I wonder why
—stuttering or crippled, maimed or cross-eyed—
I was not flung from the highest peak.

11

My soul, my soul pocked
by a 1000 resentful Carloses
that have never had the free-will
to organise their days
throughout my lifetime
& not once been able to say:
'open the door to the world,
go wherever you like,
to the north or to the south,
behind the north-wind or the southerly.'

15

Father, mother,
how much you struggled
despite the absurd Peruvian wages
to maintain some human dignity
for Pocho, Mario & me
yet after all this, I only say to myself:
'come death, so I can abandon
this humanity
& not return to it,
choosing in the end another lineage
            a cliff-face
            the face of an elm
            or an owl's.'

18

My parents, know it well:
an insect cannot be transmuted into man

but a man can be transmuted into insect!
Perhaps you never thought
when here in the world, how accidentally
oou killed some insect
which to avoid discovery by human-beings
either by day or night was anonymously lodged
in the most inaccessible & humble corner of the woods,
& you failed to realise that, as time passed,
some of your children
in spite of your thousand efforts
would become defenceless insects
so that they'd always measure up
& count as human-beings.

20

What can I do with this room,
this skin,
this brain,
if no one envies them
even a little,
father,
mother;
I wonder if it's not been in vain
that you've lent me
this room,
this skin,
this brain,
father,
mother.

Tongue-tied

Tongue-tied or stuttering,
squashed small,
    level with the heights
    I'm stretched out by my heels.

I hold it in, clamp up unwillingly,
& instead of blue fireflies
    crickets fly & spin
    in the pan of my skull,

while this darkened palate
shrunken, salivaless,
    is whipped & nagged
    by sodas & magnesias.

So I panic
like any driven mule
    & because I have children
    this is serious.

Rattled finally, fireless,
making errors from the cradle to the grave
    I'm kept going & get up daily
    sustained only by these errors.

Translation by Maureen Ahern

Juan Gonzalo Rose

The Beak of the Dove

In the next century
no one'll want—nor talk of—
doves.
We've had our bellyful of doves.
There're three types:
the dove of peace,
the dove of peace &
lastly
the dove of peace.

But perhaps
in the next century
doves won't bore us,
simply because they'll
celebrate their nuptials
in empty cities
& in the skulls time
& greed
left upon the tables.

Translated by David Tipton

From the Liturgy

Once again
we've lived through
our encounter.

We belong to the Stigma Sports Club.
If we didn't exist
blue roses would fall
on the dirty rooftops of this city;
but we
check the physics of miracles,
the oil of beatitude.

In as much
as I love you
& you love me,
assassins will take their places
in the hierarchy of great banquets.

Translated by David Tipton

Pablo Guevara

My Father

He had a big workshop. It was part of the world.
Among leather & dreams, shouts & blows
he sang & sang & drowned in life.
With Forerro & Arteche. Always with Forerro, always
with Bazetti & my father navigating the patio
the friendly liquor like an endless kingdom.
He was good & I knew it in spite of the shell
I arrived in time to caress. He was poor like many
then he grew & grew surrounded by shoes that later
became boots. Master of his trade, everything expanded
with him; the house & my money-box & this humanity.
But something was dying, slowly at first,
his faith or his courage, fragile trophies, perhaps
his enthusiasm, something was dying with the constancy
of one who has wanted too much.
And one day he was there contorted in my arms
like a worn-out shoe or a suit,
an unforgettable root remained with me.
No one was by his side. Nobody.
Outside his bedroom, friends & relatives
that, who knows, were sucking him dry.
He died alone, & with me. No one remembers him.

Translated by David Tipton

Guita Brüner

Above a rock
her troglodyte room
shines beneath the sun;
her lungs are dispersed over the whole city
where I met her one summer
on a train
coming down the Pyrenees,
a green worm
full of holiday-makers & cheeses.

I didn't swear to love her
& yet she loved me;
more laughter than you might expect
from a girl who'd lost father & mother
in the war & whose brothers smuggled
coal, cigarettes & silk-stockings.

She told me how the dawns were in Berlin
when the III Reich tried to supplant the sun,
in those days she'd seen three of her friends
carved up like fruit
& almost flayed
within an hour.

She was fourteen then
had never been invited to the cinema
& feared the worst in the most

innocuous places.
She told me she'd had to fight against
her own feelings when she'd fallen in love
with a Nazi who had the face of an angel,
his face—in her own words—
like the handsome star in some Viennese film.

And as she was telling me, she undressed;
the waves outside erased the street,
faceless pictures on the walls,
bronze gods dissolved,
the lighthouse, shipwrecks of a thousand worlds,
the rocks, the islands, the cave,
foam & our love exploding.

An Attack, 1940

Seeing the movements of cowherds
at the end of the Rhine's course,
virgins with the hint of sweaty breasts
& warm milk, of hay . . .
the motorways with their stink
of gasoline gagging the throat,
I knew that I was
once again in Rotterdam,
city lost between gigantic dykes
a crossbow's distance from the sea,
its dances of a 1000 Dutch skirts,
the plump buttocks of the local women;
yet on its doorstep
like cursed angels who won't go

the proud university students
who descended from the sky,
despoiling, buzzing,
loomed in a few seconds
with a speed admired then
–800–1000 kilometres per hour—
& strangled the city.

I should say too
that it's five centuries since
these same gentlemen
exchanged the Mediterranean basin
for that of the Atlantic . . .
Italy for the Low Countries.

I saw the door
the place still reddened
with the blood & grime of those unfortunate men
who used to return to the *Stella Mare*
—international hostel for seamen.
And the places where the merchants
tensely juggled their golden scales
in the shade of arches decked with wreathes
which triumphantly received those that returned
in triumph—the crippled & squalid
with incurable or exotic diseases,
the arrogant, self-assured & strong
after their vile bondage
to gold & its beautiful intimacy.

Like a good Latin
I settled for Eros
had my slave

for a number of dawns
while I wandered around the city
until I knew it inside out.

I saluted the statue of the crazy Erasmus
& once again relived More's marvellous Utopia.
My two sane angels!

Babylon, O Babylon

I open the scrolls of Babylon
the gardens of a 100,000 love affairs,
the 1000 doors & walls where breezes
still blow.

Soldiers with toasted skins pass close by
& I shudder. I should be invisible to them;
I scrutinise the golden images of palaces,
ssh! they're coming . . .
kings with heads
of more than human proportions,
with bovine bodies
& eagles' wings sprouting from their shoulders,
yet their features still human.
I hide in a gigantic garden pot, almost suffocated
by the giant flowers inside it
—it's odd, they're talking of religious wars,
of ambushes to kidnap a 1000 children
& of murdering someone. . . . My dream flees. . . .
I tremble so much that I invoke the night,
I want it to be so dark no one can see me

yet clear enough for me to avoid bumping into
assassins at the hour they prowl abroad.

Translated by David Tipton

Heaven & Hell

That morning their sighs
& her nakedness woke me
early, when coffee
steams; the hour that fires
the mob so the Caesars say:
outside avenues of lovers
were awaiting me,
one more day to make a conquest
& win love's crown.

In reality this is in homage
to that almost patriotic love
that resisted ambushes of laughter & of pain;
within reality & also
within the fable is that homage
to voluptuous beauty
that reminds me of Indian temples
seemingly empty but in fact full
with a 1000 eyes in an ecstasy
of the infinite & obscene
—powerful wisdom
good enough to prescribe
for sound minds in healthy bodies,
sweet little fish & whale at the same time,

in this the most transparent flank
of Europe while we followed
with centipede eyes
the manoeuvering
of the Roman legions,
& those without home or fortune
hurrying forward to abolish
once again the Empire,
I heard them say: it'll collapse
like a house built of cards.

The Bourgeois are Beasts

Between the tides
that ebb & flow
years of cruelty & stupidity
suddenly erasing cities
that people thought impregnable,
days of peace & solitude.

The Concorde Obelisk, the Chavín stone
live in my heart with their lustre.
Amid the confusion of towns
& the clamour of artillery,
my heart suffers much.
The 100 million fashions of the girls,
ostentatious uniforms;
can we in time save ourselves from stupidity?
Shall I always be prisoner,
gloomy, widowed & inconsolable
the prince of Aquitaine in his ruined tower

(as Nerval of the gas-light said
in the street of the old lantern).

How sweet & dangerous it is
to cross these venerable stones
& the even more precarious hills.
Is the world of necessity
perhaps eternal?
'The bourgeois are beasts,
the bourgeois are beasts.'
I say this every day, yet it's
because of the world's armies
that the bourgeois order survives.

I've always known this
always known it
but I have to face
the rhinoceros that's bellowed
in the Place Vendome since 1871
the year the Commune was defeated.
Between the tides
that ebb & flow
years of cruelty & stupidity.

Translated by Ena Hollis & David Tipton

From 'Civil Marriage'

I remember
at different times
hearts clustered together,

our bodies
& terrorised souls
& one morning
wounded by the beauty
of falling autumn leaves
—28th of a Danish August—
we entered the great building
—municipal hall of Frederiksberg
in the city of Copenhagen—
& were married.

I remember
in a glass bar
like an aquarium
we drank & always
hearts whirling together
saying
'skaal' 'skaal'
which means
according to the Viking toast
'skull' 'skull'
in the manner of the Incas
during the first moments of the Empire
celebrating their triumph with *chicha*
in the skulls of the conquered.

I remember
that we recorded the signs
of love with our lips
& tattoed the wineglasses,
our mouths too
& the fragile bones.
(Matter, energy,

heat & vine,
all this on earth
& in the universe too!)

I remember
that in the August wind
we went to the park in Frederiksberg
to feed the squirrels
& the black & white swans
that frequently
in honour of such humanity
went with peaceful eyes
to praise & caress
our relations in the zoo
& afterwards sailed to the island of Bornholm
just off the Polish coast
with its black lighthouses & green fields
signs of yesterday's invaders
& vast smoked-herring factories
now.

And at Helsinore
we saluted the Prince
friend of so many
& in Paris
like the Vikings
sailed in an eggshell
on a stormy sea
in front of an Algerian hotel
& later in Peru—
children, men & women
sparkling
but contorted with hunger—

where we're still living
a double existence
—sphere of necessity—
but hope one day to reach
the sphere of knowledge,
the wise & rational world
according to the elebrated
evolution of Teilhard.

I remember
that we fought each day
with millions of angels
& demons
trying to find them something
to eat & drink
trying to realise more,
to love & forgive more
—though there are those
we'll never forgive—
& always saying to ourselves
now, perhaps in a few years
light   light   light.

Rodolfo Hinostroza

To a Dead Childhood

My father's loud call like a crest of feathers
or the waters of those baths greasy to the touch. Remember?
Rusty water the colour of a smooth snake
that warmed your body so the dirt flaked off easily,
& we carried our childhood like a bright flag
between whitewashed plaster walls & the worm-eaten angels
of that sham aunt. What can I tell you about her? That
my tin sword burnt in her eyes, & that she fled
when the bonfires eroded the night of St. John.
I'd been warned, they'd repeated to me: 'Octavio, Octavio,
the river flooded its banks when you were born. We were saved
because the bells rang in warning & the family were having
a row early that morning. We climbed the hills
& the whole day watched the town die. Huascarán
looked down on us & it was then we felt its implacable whiteness.'
(We three had ceremoniously buried
in a corner of the patio, below a leaking tap, a dead canary
wrapped in my sister's plaits. The church bells brought us
to our knees & we knew that death was a beautiful word.
Yes, because we'd seen the pulpits of sickly clay
where good-natured angels dozed & knew
how to wear Sunday like a gay coat across our shoulders.)
You'll never return to that time nor find that square patio
with a date scratched in black stone. Places shrink
like that great-aunt who smelt of camphor
& the fetters of the city blot out such innocence
where your heart was anchored like a spinning song. You won't hear

the tread of father measuring the room where the portraits
blackened like dead eyelids. You'll never go back, remember now?
Now do you remember? 'Swear to me you won't tell anyone
that this white milky stuff
which the men have got gets into
the women's bellies, & then so they say
a baby's born. Like Asunción,
you remember her belly. Don't tell anyone.'
And in the porch of that house smelling of jasmin
we spied upon the Cárdenas sisters who kissed
& were kissed by the soldiers.
Then our wet-dreams stained the linen sheets
& I believed in the stories of the toothless Indian woman
who sold herbs against the evil-eye, & when I saw
that bony hand on the roof, beneath a red sky,
she laughed & cried, covering me with kisses.
O the dreams, the dreams that took the shape of cradles
in which a god-child swam between two waters. I never saw the sea
& all was solid to the touch, like that family
bred between hills & stars in times as distant as
the language that the servants spoke. Pedro Granados
carried me piteously. His youngest children were killed
in a landslide like a rain of stones & mud & I'd heard
that on certain days he lost his memory. And the beautiful
handwriting
of our mother, & her hands that drew cathedrals in adobe
& the forbidden leather-trunks where books trembled
like frightened fish.
Why does one cry? Tell me the things one cries about
when you have solid parents & saliva gags your mouth
& you've received an old silver-spoon
& you went for walks in moonlight, through a cedar-wood,
trying to control the urge to piss. Why does one cry,

when in the burnt-siena afternoons you've lit the candles
to your patron saints, when nothing's fallen except perhaps
the nest of some bird in a puddle. Why does one cry then,
when the days close like bows & the world
is a word that leaps & itches on the tongue?
You remember, exiled by your tremendous sleepwalking,
the open drains of the city that fed the gold river,
the cattle-troughs next to the cemetery
marked by enormous stones like the tears of a god,
where we found talismans & crooked sticks
that flooded your forehead with majesty?
                                                            People, their names,
revealed by chattering monkeys beneath a holiday sky.
                                                            Kid-skin drums
distancing things & things of bronze
towards the scarlet cities, while my mother, participant
of my dreams, waited for some succulent fruit I'd seen
in the market, next to the painted saucepans, at the back of the stall.
I'll talk about this destiny, today, which I watched growing
like a great plaster arch in the house, when my shadow fled
like a dead flame. And of the grief that hung
from monotonous fingers, & I say you can be especially tender
when you have a tin sword
& the stars come & shorten the distances
in the grey look.
                              Because I remember
that I had all this & I saw a white mule resting
beneath a January sun & heard the adults comment
upon the news of a certain distant war. And the bishop's move
& the lazy king kept me absorbed hour after hour
in the perfume of midmorning, beneath the January sun,
waiting for my father's next brilliant move.

Othello's Report

'. . . Once in Aleppo,
yes, it was in Aleppo where I disgraced myself with this
circumcised Turk:
I girded him with his own saliva, & his purple tongue spat
prayers, & thus
I saved my life. This life which was worth so little, & which
today weighs in your hands
like an ebony coffer, Signorina.
Though I were to fall
bowled over by a dream of peace
broken by the rattles of war, nothing would be lost if I didn't
lose you.
Though I fall on the bitter planks of memory
& choose the final experience, & meet what is only a wet bird
& the end & sense of this journey is misguiding
like the rusty coin of something that never happened, nothing
will have been lost
If I've succeeded in loving you.
"Moor! Who have you fought for? Moor!
For what have you fought?" the idle horsemen shouted
while I was talking to you. And in truth, Signorina, after this
ferocious flight of a wounded arrow, I've turned round
to see who I've been dealing with, & have met no one. But
your men
spit from hidden places when I pass, & mine deny me, & that
silent
impulse to greatness that raised me from slaves & galleys

has gone, & it's as if suddenly, in the middle of night
the noise of the sea should stop, waking us,
& icy fear & premonition trespass like spiders in the throat.
                    Towards Cyprus once
an insolent blond told me I smelt like a rat, I had only time to
    wound him
before they threw me off the ship, & I was on my own again
because of my smell, my skin, & this look that drives away owls.
                    I remained alone
after telling my painful story
of brutality & misery, of fears, of phlegm, & a passion for love
above skin & beneath it
tense as a tattoo, Signorina . . .'

The Night

These days we're advised
against modesty & you're warned right away
that the essence of things is elusive. Cloudy
desire stirs in the hearts of the men.
Here's the barmaid. If she's not in a bad mood
she'll permit everything tonight.
We'll invite her down to the beach. Talking to her
make her undress, she must have
a great body. You can see the incest
in her pallid cheeks; her father, a bit of a mule,
started her off. Yet despite that
we'll listen to her & maybe she'll murmur
sweet or bitter things like hazel nuts. And then
drink our wine & with the beat of the waves
on her thighs she'll be fucked by all of us. And feel good

tonight. It'll be our night without let or hindrance.
Ah, he's got aroused, that anonymous boy
with the tough chest. If we taunt him
with sarcasm, whip his sex with thorns,
& prevent him from looking at the sea, he'll grow old
tonight. (We're dealing with a shy bride
but still a peasant's daughter. She imagines her brother's
chest & trembles; dreams of a noisy gathering
around a table & of a quiet wedding night
with a slight breeze, a gentle smile, a sweet zephyr.
But she'll feel the friction
of a hot animal prick & hesitate.) We advise the anonymous boy
with the hard-on
the best way of doing it
so that she'll not struggle longer than fifteen minutes.
Tonight the bellowing of the stags'll echo among the trees.
We'll drink. Some of us'll wander off to look
at the glittering sea & will feel like touching the moon
with out feet. (We'll look at the boy with the broken back,
the boy with a bundle of firewood
or the old woman with the walking-stick & perhaps
we'll stop & imagine it was a Soviet spaceship.
Lovers of progress will blaze with words & doubtless attract
the taciturn hero to their circle of listeners. Later
the discussions on being will begin. The ontologists
in moorish hats will defend their abstract metaphysics.
They'll prove that the spirit of wine rises in our eyes.
Something as intermittent as a chameleon will make us doubt
for a moment, then we'll resume our interrupted coitus.)
Some of us, skilful in the art, have brought along guitars.
Let's sing then. An old or new song? Someone suggests
A song of 17th century Provence. (It'll smell
of precious stones & the stable, one supposes. Let's listen.)

'I'm going off to the war
but the damp stone
of my heart
remains with you' ! . . . etc . . .
Tonight we need more liquor. Let someone go
& buy it. Let's chip into the kitty so a little group
can go to the tavern. And they better return soon.
Meanwhile we'll hear a confused conversation
about a recent book which is itself confused. The sea's
calming down a little. The naked tavern's so close to the sea
they could wash their glasses in it. The back part shines
in the moonlight. Perhaps tonight she'll fall in love
with someone she used to go out with a long time ago.
The moment's come to light a huge bonfire
& make it blaze with the verses of these young poets
who appear drunk. We'll pick up logs of wood
stained by the moon or driftwood from ships
that must have shipwrecked in these latitudes. All
will feel a little heated, even those warmed between
the thighs of a woman. We'll behave like civilised people
tonight.
At this point some bitterness'll enter
our hearts & someone'll begin to hum a tune again—
an old Provençal song from the 17th century. The women
are tired & in a corner they talk about the night's
events. Some have had orgasms like those of a mare,
others a rabbit's & others weak spasms like water.
No one's paid any attention to the new wine.
Now we feel
like listening to the bland wisdom of some old man
& this surprises us because even living overtime we worry
about the future of mankind.
A metallurgist gets to his feet & says he's thirsty.

A civil-servant also says something about a dry throat.
(In spite of fatigue the tendency is to violence.
Words like *fuck* & *cunt* begin to fly around
& echo along the beach. Shit
adheres to names & each one of us feels a little guilty.
We've sown shock in the eyes of the old man.
He mutters something that sounds like *salvation* & leaves.
Our women's
vaginas seep with juice again. And they remember
that this is our long night.)
It's true the wine is cloudy
& that it'll never have the freshness of the dawn, but it's sure
too, that we know how to prolong the night to incredible extremes
& that the lucid wailing of a cat & the crowing
of the cocks accompany us; that they've encroached upon the night,
our condoms hanging from the trees
& our beautiful bottles sunk in the sand.

Antonio Cisneros

Paracas

Since early morning
the water has been rising between the red backs
of the shells

& fragile-footed gulls
chewing the small tidal animals

until they're swollen like boats
spread out beneath the sun.

Only rags
& skulls of the dead tell us

that beneath these sands
our ancestors were buried in droves.

Pachacamac

Even the earth between my fingers
& this tough straw, sadden me.
Here the builder went down on his knees
in the sand, or chased off
boys with sunburnt backs,
marauders of the reservoirs & terraces.
The rafts haven't come yet
nor the old men with fuzzy caps

& necklaces of teeth. Only
a few green & wrinkled lizards
sleep in the walls, & piss
almost daily on the hide
of the wise builder.

Translated by David Tipton

Workers of the Sun's Land

They knew
the sun
could eat
not even
one shred
of green corn
but avoided
the fire,
the spear
in
under their
ribs.

Ancient Peru

With *huarango* branches
they scared off the flies
that swarmed
above the breasts of the dead

On the temple stones
old chieftains made love
with the widows & a red sun
scorched
their children's bones.

The Dead Conquerors

I

They came by water
these men with blue flesh
who trailed beards
& never slept
in order to rob each other blind.
Dealers in crosses
& brandy, who
founded their cities
with a temple.

II

During that summer of 1526
the rain tumbled down
on their daily work, & heads
& no one repaired
the rusty old armour.
Black fig trees grew
between the pews & altars,
while on the rooftiles

sparrows broke their beaks
silencing the bells.
Afterwards in Peru
no one, though master
in his own house,
could move around
without treading upon the dead,
nor sleep next to white chairs
or swamps
without sharing his bed
with some cancerous relative.
Shit upon by scorpions & spiders
few survived their horses.

Question of Time

I

A bad deal you made, Almagro.
From no stone
of the Atacama could you beg for bread
nor gold from its sand.
And the sun's tinopeners
exposed your soldiers
to the hunger
of a cloud of vultures.

II

In 1964,
where your bearded eyes

saw only red cactus,
other vultures reap
forests
so deep in metals
that a hundred Spanish armadas
transporting them
would have shipwrecked beneath the sun.

Translated by David Tipton

Prayers of a Repentant Gentleman

I *When the devil haunts me,*
proclaiming your penances

Lord, rust my forks
& medals, rot my teeth,
drive my barber crazy,
strike dead
the servants in their beds
but free me from the devil.
Smelling of rum, his hair matted
he comes up to my house
& I've surprised him
naked & wrinkled
rolling among the geraniums.
I'm a little fat, Lord,
& am awaiting your penances,
but not too many
or too rigorous.
I've aged in battles

& my idols are dead.
Now, scare off the devil,
wash those geraniums
& my heart too, &
may there be peace, amen.

2 *When the devil is exorcised,*
Communion from the Bishop

Lord, I feel your blood
raging in my veins,
your flesh, a bed
of consecrated bread,
comforts me,
& your love through penance
is sweeter
than idle vestments
& taverns.
Iron, you've lavished
favours upon me, &
moreover my recent piety
rails against the Bishop.

Lord, your saintly body in his hands
—the same that have sequestered
candelabras
& exchanged them for wine—
is broken into crumbs.
Hands that
between confessions
have wandered over
the bodies of widows

& boys.
Lord, split his fingers,
wash his eyes with salt,
let the rats
gnaw his rings
& crimson mitre,
corral him
with your warriors
so that the devil
cannot escape
from his soul.

3 *On the death of the Bishop, who was truly of your ilk*

Lord, your accomplice
the bishop is dead.
Some old women
are weeping
among muted bells
& his debtors
observe joyful
mourning.
Lord, he was truly
your friend,
& at the business table
you worried
about his deals

In the old days
you stuffed your chests
with Abel's things.

I also suspect
you knowingly
sent Jesus
to the slaughter-house.

Túpac Amaru Relegated

There are liberators
with long sideburns
who saw the dead & wounded brought back
after the battles. Soon their names
were history & the sideburns
growing into their old uniforms
proclaimed them founders of the nation.

Others with less luck have taken up
two pages of text
with four horses & their death.

Translated by David Tipton

Tarma

Sun on the walls, the roofs
swaying among branches,
the tangled gorse in my shirt,
blackbirds in my shoes,
cobbled streets of eucalyptus
climbing towards the hills

& yet
the flies & the dead
need neither
fig trees nor gorse, nor the shade
of the clustered willows.

Three Testimonies of Ayacucho

From a Soldier

After the battle
there was nowhere to pile up
the dead,
so dirty & hollow-eyed, scattered
over the grass like leavings
from this tough fight,
the swollen & yellowed heroes
littered among the stones
& disembowelled horses
were stretched out beneath the dawn.

I mean that dead comrades
are the same
as any other edible meat
after a battle, & soon
a hundred brown birds
flocked upon their corpses
until the grass was clean.

From a Mother

Some soldiers who were drinking brandy
have told me that now this country
is ours.
They also said
I shouldn't wait for my sons.
So I must
exchange the wooden chairs
for a little oil & some bread.

The land is black as dead ants,
the soldiers said it was ours.
But when the rains begin
I'll have to sell
the shoes & ponchos
of my dead sons.

Some day I'll buy a long-haired mule
& go down to my fields
of black earth
to reap the fruit
of these broad dark lands.

From a Mother
again

My sons & the rest of the dead still
belong to the owner of the horses
& the owner of the lands, & the battles.

A few apple trees grow among their bones
& the tough gorse. That's how they fertilise

this dark tilled land.
That's how they serve the owner
of war, hunger, & the horses.

Description of a Plaza, a Monument & Allegories in Bronze

The horse, a liberator
of green bronze whitened
by birdshit
Three fat girls:
Country, Liberty
& a little tilted,
Justice. Next to
the horse's ass: Sovereignty,
Fraternity & Prudence
(a big belly & laurel-wreaths
open in her hands).
Modesty & Charity
fanning the liberator—
wrapped in his flag
of green & white—
with leafy branches.
Archangels
with abundant horns.
A plaque
with the name of the dead man,
the mayor in office,
the signatures
of the sponsors,
the battles, the president

& the bishops. A spiked rail,
rusted daily by the dogs,
round the paths & steps
for the use of beggars.
Wooden benches, geraniums, other girls
their hair greenish white: Hope,
Beauty & Chastity, &
at the back of the group, Spring,
worm-eaten privet, &
Democracy. Almost daily too
assault-troops,
black truncheons, green helmets
whitened by birdshit.

Translated by David Tipton

Karl Marx, died 1883 aged 65

I can still remember my great aunt's old house & that pair
    of etchings:
'A gentleman at the tailor's,' & 'Great Military parade in Vienna.'
Days when nothing bad could happen. Everyone carried a
    rabbit's foot tied to their belts.
My great aunt too—20 years old in a straw hat for the sun
    scarcely worrying about more
than keeping her mouth shut & her legs closed.
The men were of goodwill & kept their noses clean.
Anarchists could only be found in the music-halls, crazy &
    bearded, wrapped in scarves.
What summers! What autumns!
Eiffel built a tower that said: 'Man has reached this height.'
    Another etching:

'Virtue, Love & Zeal protecting decent families.'
And yet it was less than 20 years since old Marx had been put
six feet under grass—tough & stiff, fit only for golf-courses.
The wreaths & coffin rested 3 times at the foot of the hill
& then he was buried
next to the tomb of Molly Redgrove ('bombed by the enemy in
1940 & rebuilt').
And old Karl melting & grinding different metals in the pot
while his children jumped from the towers of *Der Spiegel*
to the islands of *The Times*
& his wife boiled onions & things didn't go well & later
they did & then came the Place Vendome & Lenin & a whole lot
of revolts, then
the ladies were scared of more than a pat on the ass & gentlemen
suspected
that the steam-engine was no longer the symbol of universal
happiness.
'That's the way it was & I'm in your debt, old spoilsport.'

Chronicle of Lima

'To allay the doubt
that grows tormentously,
remember me, Hermelinda,
remember me.'
('Hermelinda', Creole Waltz)

Here're recorded my birth & marriage
the death
of grandfather Cisneros & grandfather Campoy.
Here too is recorded the best of my works

—a boy & beautiful.
All the roofs & monuments remember my battles
against the King of the Dwarfs, & the dogs
in their fashion celebrate the memory of my remorse.
(I was also
fed up with the base wines &
without a trace of shame or modesty was master
of the Ceremony of the Frying.)
O city
maintained by the skulls & customs of kings who were
the dullest & ugliest of their time.
What was lost or gained
between these waters?

I try to remember the names of the heroes, of the
great traitors.
Remember me, Hermelinda, remember me.

The mornings're a little colder
but you'll never be certain of the seasons
—it's almost 3 centuries since they chopped down the woods
& the fields were destroyed by fire.
The sea's close,
Hermelinda,
but you can never be sure of its rough waters,
its presence
save for the rust on the windows;
the broken masts,
immobile wheels
& the brick-red air.
But the sea's very close,
& the horizon extended & suave.
Think of the world

as a half-sphere—half-an-orange, for example—
      on 4 elephants,
on the 4 columns of Vulcan,
                                    & the rest is fog.
A white furry veil protects you from the open sky.
You should see
                    4 19th century houses
                    9 churches from the 16th, 17th & 18th centuries,
                    for $2\frac{1}{2}$ soles, a catacomb too,
where noble bishops & lords, their wives & children
shed their hides.
                    The Franciscans
inspired by some chapel in Rome
—so the guide'll tell you—converted
the tough ribs into dahlias, marigolds & forget-me-nots
—*Remember, Hermelinda*—the shinbones & skulls
      into Florentine arches.
(And the jungle of cars, a sexless snake of no known species,
      beneath the red traffic-lights.)
                    There's also a river.
Ask about it, & they'll tell you this year
      it's dried up.
Praise its potential waters, have faith in them.
On the sandy hills
barbarians from the south & east have built
a camp that's bigger than the whole city, & they
      have other gods.
(Arrange some convenient alliance.)
This air—they'll tell you—
turns everything red & ruins most things
      after the briefest contact.
Thus
your plans & your efforts'll become

rusty needles
before even their points emerge.
And this mutation—*remember Hermelinda*—
doesn't depend on your will.
The sea revolves in channels of air,
the sea revolves,
it is the air.
You cannot see it.

Moreover I was at the quayside in Barranco
picking out round flat pebbles to skim across the water.
I had a girl with slim legs. And a job.
And this memory, pliant as a pontoon-bridge,
anchors me
to the things I've done
& the infinite number of things left undone,
to my good, or bad luck, to things I've neglected.
To what was lost or gained
between these waters.
Remember, Hermelinda, remember me.

Between the Quay of San Nicolás & the Sea

'*For you, my son,*
I write of what we were.'
(Horace Gregory)

There's a little sun still, the cables creak
& the water
sways once again between the white stakes.

In San Nicolás I've seen a boy & girl embracing

against a red crane
The wind blew continuously from the south
howling like demons.
Who's calling me? Did I switch off the kitchen light
or forget one of my books?
And the reply like the applause of the gods
never comes.
She was slim & moved her hands under
the boy's black sweater.
Sea of San Nicolas, with its oily waves.

Day surprised me within the walls of Jerusalem
& in debt to my brother,
the signal from Delphi gave little warning.
O fucking remorse!
I'd not set my house in order that day.
The music of the dead jars against a red crane.
Forgive me.
What iron-filings collect in our hearts.
Forgive me.
The boy & girl clambered up a mountain of tin
& switched on the light.
The Great Bear was bright & its fuzzy tail
hung from the sky.
Forgive me.
I strolled along the wharfs, shapeless
as a dead jelly-fish
& the wind continued to blow over you
our young baby,
a banana peel where flies are feasting.
Forgive me.
Later the sirens of San Juan & Acari wailed
& at seven we put to sea.

Some sun still, the cables creak & the water
sways once more between the white stakes.
No birds fly overhead, my Diego, & before
night closes in I think of you.
Forgive me. Forgive her.

Translated by David Tipton

Loneliness 2

'Friend, I'm reading your old poems on the north terrace.
The oil lamp flickers.
How sad to be lettered & a clerk.
I'm reading about the free & flexible rice fields. I raise my eyes
& can only see
the official books, the expenses of the province, the yellowed
accounts
of the Empire.'

It was last summer & that night he reached my hotel on
Sommerard Street
I'd been waiting for him two years.
I hardly remember anything of our conversation.
He was in love with an Arab girl & that war
—the Fox Dayan's—was even more painful to him.
'Sartre is old & doesn't know what he's doing,' he told me &
also said
that Italy had made him happy with its empty beaches, sea
urchins & green water
full of fat glistening bodies. 'Like the baths at Barranco,'
a summerhouse built at the turn of the century & a dish of crabs.

He'd stopped smoking. And literature was no longer his trade.
The oil lamp flickered four times.
Silence grew strong as an ox.
And so to salvage something I told him about my room & my
    neighbours in London
about the Scotswoman who'd been a spy in both wars,
about the doorman—a pop-singer
& having nothing more to tell him, I damned the English &
    shut up.

The oil lamp flickered again
& then his words shone brighter than some beetle's back
& he spoke of the Great March, the Blue River with its turgid
    waters
about the Yellow River & its cold currents & we imagined
toughening ourselves by running & jumping along the seashore
doing without music or wine, relying
for wisdom on our eyes only,
& none of this seemed like a mirage in the desert.
But my gods are weak & I doubted
And the young stallions were lost behind walls
& he did not return that night to the hotel on Sommerard Street.
Obstinate & slow gods, trained to gnaw at my liver every morning
Their faces are dark, ignorant of revelation.
'Friend, I'm on the island that's going under north of the Channel
& I'm reading your poems,
the rice fields are full of the dead
& the oil lamp flickers.'

I'm getting out
& going some 30 kilometres towards the coast

I'm getting out
& going some 30 kilometres towards the coast
where one day I saw tall dark grass
reaching to the sea,   & my only joy
will be that grass brushing my ears,
my only comfort those easy waters,
I'll just stretch out on the wet sand, shoeless,
close my eyes,   & shut my heart
like the saltwater snails,
the hard red ones.

Javier Heraud

A Guerrilla's Word

Because my country is beautiful
like a sword in the air
& bigger now & even
still more beautiful,
I speak out & defend it
with my life.
I don't care what traitors
say
we've blocked the way
with thick tears
of steel.
The sky is ours.
Ours our daily bread.
we've sown & harvested
the wheat & the land,
ours too
& always ours
the sea,
the jungles
& the birds.

Translated by Maureen Ahern

A Guerrilla's Goodbye

One afternoon he said to his girl
'I'm going, the rainy season's here,
everything's all washed up.
Life's got me by the throat.
I can't stand any more oppression
while assassin's bullets
are killing my brothers in
the mountains.'
Adiòs. I'm off to the hills
with the guerrillas.
He said goodbye & left
& one day he was up there on top
alongside the guerrillas.

Translated by Maureen Ahern

Summer

Drumrolled gusts of love
shake my heart & eyes.
(It's the light of life &
days. It's the penalty
of death & night.)
I reap & sow the seeds
of love: a

way between nights
darkened by
wine,
I question the earth
& the hills,
I tear up jungles
of hate & riot:
what are afternoons
aside of peace,
what are hills
aside of dreams.
what are rivers
aside of tears,
what's a smile,
a wail,
a shudder,
a
face
a
hand,
if day by day
grass
dies
in the fields,
& day by day
the trees
of love
& silence
crash down
in their nights?

Translated by Maureen Ahern

From 'Earth Poems'

3

I want two geraniums
to sprout from my eyes,
two white roses from my forehead,
& from my mouth
(whence
my words spring)
a strong perennial cedar
that'll shade me when
I burn inside & out,
that'll give me a breeze
when the rain drenches my bones.
Pour water on me every
morning, fresh from
the nearby river,
so that I'll be fertiliser
for my own vegetables.

4

Everything's wood, the condors,
the masks, the rivers
& the dark honeysuckle.
The trees have roots

in the ground, in the pavement,
in the sidewalk, in frozen
bread, & even in the tree
itself.
Cement is a tree,
gold is tree,
tree pure iron
& wood the crystals.
Everything's a slender root,
the foundations of the vine,
the buttons of the necktie,
the buckles of my wrinkled
guts. Everything's wood, the
dawn in your sleepy eyes,
the fingers of my clenched
hands, the sun in its turbulent
setting.

5

Everything's the colour of leaves,
green, skyblue, bright
yellow.
Everything comes falling down
with the same rhythm
as the leaves.
No! Don't look for
green among the boots,
the green of the unattainable pastures,
the green in your tangled eyes.
Everything will clarify later.
Later on it will be time

for hanging leaves,
& leaves trodden
in the ground,
for leaves in bud
& in their burrow.

6

Sugar tastes like fresh
ants,
spiders' webs in the ground,
wet flowers between naked rivers.
There's sugar in my
sweetened side,
ashtrays with burnt cigarettes,
the arms
of narrow chairs.
Sugar can change the world,
turn the saltiest thing
sweet,
turn the urine
to sugar
& the eyes
burning in death.
It can enter the blood,
weaken the world,
step on it with a full mouth
in its sweet burn-out end.

Translated by Maureen Ahern

A New Journey

I must travel again
towards
the white jungles
that're waiting for me.

Towards the same winds
& orange groves
must my huge feet
eat up the land
& my eyes caress
the vines in the fields.

Lone & total journey:
it's so hard to leave
everything behind.
It's so hard to live
between cities,
a street,
a trolley,
everything piles up
& only the
eternal season
of disillusion survives.

You can't stroll
along the sands
if there're oppressor snails
& submarine spiders.

And yet,
walking a little,
turning to the left
you reach the jungles
& the rivers.
It's not that I want
to get away from life,
it's just that I have
to get closer to death.

It's not that I want
to insure my steps;
it's just that every so often
they spring an ambush on us
& occassionally steal
our letters,
every so often
they trap us
with deceit.

It's better: I recommend it:
to get away for a while
from the turmoil
& get to know
the untracked jungles.

Translated by Maureen Ahern

Marco Martos

Our House

In galleons, on war-horses, with their lances
& helmets—illiterate the first lot—
they arrived in waves
& in this house which was ours,
right here, they laid down the law.
They were the kings,
they had the weapons.
And when in the end they went
after some deaths, shootings & treaties,
as a legacy, they left us
their blood & the cross, a language & nothing;
the house divided
in spoonfuls.
Now neighbours, invited guests,
starving beggars, all claim us as their own.

Translated by David Tipton

Quijote

I've spent the whole year
looking at the girls' faces
& dreaming of their asses,
believing in rewards
which stretched out

like chewing-gum
in endless expectation.
Totting up the year's account
I don't mind wasting 300 days
playing the fool,
but it riles me
as much as it did
playing the gentleman
in the 12th century.
I swear & perjure myself
in the lances of love
but I'm going to try a new line:
serious unsociable men
that's what the girls want.

Translated by David Tipton

From 'Casa Nuestra'

3

Sometimes I visit the city
& do what everyone does:
walk through the streets
climb on the trams
buy newspapers
get bored
go to the movies.

Quixotic animal
I try to enjoy myself

with very little money.
Babylon devours me.
Often I'm insulted
but cannot defend myself;
they are too many.

Suicide smiles at me
from the balconies
of the skyscrapers
but I take no notice
& return to the country.

4

Don't you forget it:
I'm a cicada & I sing
& glancing towards the stars
I ask one favour:
find me a friend
who'll give me
bread & wine
a house & easy work
for the hard days
that're coming.
I know that it's February
but I'm a modern cicada
& I'm becoming cautious.

Translated by David Tipton

Politics

It isn't in my bones
to drift with the current;
the smiles that those who pass
demand from me
I transform into grimaces.
I admit to liking parades
beautiful flags
triumphant festivities
but from there to other things
distances exist,
distances, the apple-tree.
In the face of oblivion
rightly or wrongly
I show off my Roman lineage
—one of the evil Romans—
& because of this don't change.

With obsolete
interest
I read books & magazines
on the social question
but don't visit
the shantytowns
nor want to teach illiterates
to read & write.
Full of doubts
I write what I like

for those who want
my friendship.
What can it matter
to all the rest
what I think:
I don't talk about small boats
nor go in for
intellectual games
I write
to calm
my nerves,
almost from necessity.

Translated by David Tipton

Julio Ortega

Fishermen

In the mantle of dawn dreamy boats
cleaving through blue cotton,
their shadows towards the wharf
as the fishermen scattered a shoal of fish
    awaking sluggishly.
In Lima they asked me about these men
—Saturday night, the honeyed lamp, smokey bars
& sweaty light that yellowed the walls,
the sound of grimy money
& the turmoil in the brothels,
Saturday & the oily clamour of their voices—
many questions about this.
Why were they so curious about my background?
A pool of sun-dust, the restless sea
beneath their feet, a kind of creaking
from the decks, & the waves of this cabin
their high crests without a cross or flowers.
    How to answer?
Terrible men, I'd heard, men lost
between the clink of coins, in the chaos
of alcohol, & always money
exchanged from the sea, a forbidden world:
questions that veiled green envy.
    That time, Pedro in Chimbote
emerged from his flesh, teetering like a stalk
on an intimate wind from land,
his arms swimming along the street

& his lips tightly-sealed,
laughing like a solitary fish
at the strange sound of some word.
    The psychedelic rhythm
of the whirling fair, circus music,
trapeze artists through the air;
the carnival & its streaked wind; boys
laughing in orange fire.

    Words in Lima lie,
stooped towards the earth we cast long shadows
& only the dust—the yellow money;
    no other music tints the air.

From what nakedness, or regions of the sun,
    what vertigo of sea,
    from what first words
    have we fallen? Anchors of night
neither sun nor sea permit us flowers.
    (Pedro sometimes came
& left the brothels quickly,
paid for taxis, American clothes, & taunted
those people, that he said, only worked to die.)
    Neither money nor rage: boys being born
one day & grown-up the next, flowers, striplings,
fresh water in their hands, & this
    is simple. Bronzed by the sun
they quickly change the course of rivers.
Now ask about their misery,
the dark humidity that persecutes them, the ash?
    Here the knife sinks in,
the sharp edge of the sea's stopped, & again I hear
the thick sound of coins clinking in the night,

cold arithmetic out of the steamy sweat.
You'd have to sketch the jaded faces
of avaricious owners, the ash left over from the fire,
the top country in the world's fishmeal market,
anonymous statistics
The dogs at the fair wagging their tails
await the night: starving they poke around
with the torpor of the lonely, are reduced in number,
& there're laws for this.
(Pedro drinks suavely
& looks at his friends like tired lamps
who hiccup in the vacuum of night;
the owners, he says, & there ends this orange time
& its odour of fish-scales, where
the nets seem to symbolise some dream.)

Judge this scene,
the music of a flamboyant time
the quick eyes that gleam with the sea
& the investments of money & guilt
—judge this scene,
you delicate & anonymous readers.

Awaking warm from sleep they still come
along the misty asphalt
& inside
surrounded by swollen foam tempt the sun
sing & chew
the stems of milky pollen,
branches that flash like a forest
of children.

Memory of Dust & Light

The sun comes up: a day in June. Time sinks
in the keen shine of its yielding waters
a day in June, a time in June,
Chimbote opens its hands,
        a throw of the dice:
houses emerge as white & greenish metal-sheets,
        leaves filed by the wind.
The dust blew up early, fanned
& heated their coals & irons,
        one day in June
in the broad sweep of the sun, clusters
of fishermen gathered like steaming pools,
rippled by the dusty tremor of the wind,
        the sound of the sea,
& on the corners the day flamed dryly.

I opened the door early. 'The strike's been broken.'
The streets splayed out cleanly like a pack of cards.
        Groups of men churned up the dust,
the port's closed before their eyes,
a day in June like a leaf falling from a tree.
'The strike ruins us!' I heard the moan of the wind
trapped between staccato shouts & the beat of my pulse
the pauses & rhythm of the flesh.
    On the Galvez bridge—a swirl of wind—
fishermen & police, fibre to fibre restraining themselves.
On the Galvez bridge, from a mound of dust,

I saw the greenish-lemon sea, the smooth grey islands
swaying on the water. I saw words teetering
like feathers, & the weight of the sun,
the harsh measure of light in these faces.

    Groups jostled together in the wide avenue,
dark heads bobbing & moving from side to side
in speech, the ground reflecting them,
    bodies clustered together, black heads
& hands raised high, struggling above the dark water
    one day in June.
Faces oscillate in the heat-haze,
they're here as one man whose backbone I know:
they advance along the bridge, forward.
Closing the bridge, the police closing it,
what sort of men are they behind their
green uniforms & machine-guns,
chopping down the sun, green masks
    in Chimbote, by the sea,
    one day in June?
Ah men of my home-town, I've seen a face
& its silky blood, its small sea spilling out,
its saliva & empty hands, a mutilated river,
    one day in June.
They moved forward. Towards the bridge. Up.
Between two shores, enclosed by sharp light
the advanced. Towards the bridge. Forward.
Their shouts like glistening oil in my head,
cries burnt in my flesh, swollen in the haze,
their voices rosy pasta
or gritty milk in my hands,
    one day in June.
Men of my town, a bullet's entered

my ribs, the blow of a face in the dust,
the earth yielding smoothly
    to the sweat that jewels it:
it ran in my veins, opened my hands
    & in the burning dust
my body followed it, breathed twice
    in the churned up dust
    one day in June.
Four times the reddish cloud fell back beaten:
    leaving a sediment behind,
four faces, bellies, necks in pools of blood,
    the sound of their voices
    extinguished.
    Night falls on the water.
A branch of boats sways in the cold darkness,
the low murmur of the sea comes to me,
    the subtle lap
    of the nearest wave from the beach.
Then I saw between the houses, the dense echo of the wind
staining the mirrors with its warm breath,
the women withdrawing into their yellow acid,
    it lingered in the homefires
leaving its fine pollen.
    The whole night vigil was kept,
neither heroes nor gods, in the corner of houses
enveloped by the slow pulse of blood
    & sweet breathing
—in their black homes they'll not feel cold,
    neither heroes nor gods,
four fishermen killed, extinguished
like the shadows of trees in a terrible river.
    And they didn't feel cold
but in the morning journeyed on the trembling water

in the arms of young *morenos*, floated
on the pallid crowd, before the open houses,
a pregnant river cleaving the silence
they journeyed over the dust stained by fire.
        O heavy heart,
what silence the slow crowd pours out,
town of my bones, a throw of whitish dice,
houses filed by the wind,
your brown bodies smoothly absorbed
    like wine spilt on the ground:
death passes & submits to life,
the two shores merge in a single line,
my flesh's filled with a foaming echo
    in the scorching sun
        one day in June.

Translated by David Tipton

October

In the half-empty City Hall—
(Romeo, Juliet & the darkness)—
we heard the sax of Fausto Papeti
during the late-night show.
O so strange in an artificial paradise
smoking by your side
& intervals with the smoke of music.
O so odd in my country
a Jewish girl with long glossy hair
& a suave Czech film,
I was smoking by your side

during the 5 minute intermission
& one new year's eve
we drank vodka & grapefruit juice
as this same sax drenched us
in a cascade of heat & darkness,
O so strange in this tough paradise.
Intervals like noisy anchors
& my beatup feelings, my heart,
retreating to a gentle cove, a haven
like driftwood or desires
beaten up yet sumptuous.
Paradise with a stranger
& the sax or the smoke of my cigarette
in an artificial night
by your side during another pause,
O the dark shadows of love
& the curse of this story
in a cold half-empty theatre
with few people.

Translated by David Tipton

Sound of Water

Time has a certain rhythm
like contemporary-style furniture
white & weightless as the summer.
(The actors took their place beneath the amber light
above time that murmurs in the stalls
as the curtain falls & rises.
O the sad refinement of the senses

in the muscles of an actor
        exhilarated by applause.)

How does the soldier return to war
after promising everything to his girl?

Time with its amber weight
is a licor poured into a glass
or the movement of hair
or perhaps making out
in the cramped space of a Volkswagen
or in the tension of the skin
after a morning swim at San Bartolo.
Remember the boredom of moving house
& the hospital's visiting hours
& a certain tranquil August.
(at eight the telephone in my pension rang)
or the time we spent in parks
or kissing in dark corners of half-finished buildings
or waiting for service at the cafes on Saturdays.
Butterflies' wings—O memories flowing
in the sound of water—& at midday
we ate grilled chicken & chips
& I brought all my books
& the TV shouted out the news,
O those experiences we've shared
through which we'll always have
something to talk about together.
Quick memories in the amber weight of time
or a village of bourgainvillea
a house remembered from my youth.

Translated by David Tipton

Report for Isolda

I

Last night, December 24th 1966
we opened the presents—a blouse for mum
slippers for me (a fragile peace in homes
lit by innocence & a moment's calm)
& for you a rubber doll that squeaked.
We ate mince-pies
& on television listened to the phoney promises
smiling irrelevancies too absurd for anger;
sliced the ham & pork
while kids in the building fired caps
celebrating gunpowder in their ignorance.
At the same time a shantytown in Da Nang, South Vietnam
was obliterated by a shelling
—(wrenched screams   smashed heads
brains spilt)—the villagers stunned
at their Christmas Eve tables by a North American plane
exploding upon their small bodies
in which love lived. The pilot
& over a hundred people
who neither chose Christmas
nor a sky scabbed by planes
were killed.
Milk spilt on their tables
ash   the split brain of that land
a hundred surprised men.

And you my daughter remember
those dead by fire & gasoline
killed by error in an erring time.

2

That same night—last night
in mudchoked Florence, Paul VI said mass.

—Let us weep, he said, with the nations
that are suffering, for Florence, created by artists,
has been bitten to the quick—

And he said that Art treasures were not mere objects
of pride & contemplation but inspired the search
for universal & immortal values.
            Rebirth is a grand word.
Art in Florence has been attacked before
by water, its roots slashed;
the city blocked by crude mud.

But, Florence, it's useless to mourn
for there will be no rebirth;
other cities will carry your torch
through the world in the future;
the birds no longer sing for you.

The Pope in a red ermine-lined cape
surveyed the muddy streets & prayed,
I hear him here where St. Peter shook off the dust—
Rebirth, said this Peter, and—
Art will raise its values like tents

on a battlefield . . . But you, my daughter,
remember that here too we're trying
to sow seeds among thorns,
create signs that'll explode & fire
worn-out bodies, hunger
that's like dust in our houses—remember
our thirst & the mud that's everywhere
like a new god on this earth.

Translated by David Tipton

My Country

The young men for example of the nineteen hundreds
& before the 'thirties passed through patios & drawing-rooms
between orange sunshades
or read through lists of mourners at funerals
smiling with approval at their moustaches because they were
    adjusted
to the times & the sure progress of the country.
But there were others on horseback
who I know endured heavy rain in the fields
& they say the earth seemed to recede
& between the valley & the coast the fruit ripened
a slow dark liquor descending to the shore,
& along the length of the country
hardening with the children, quick deals, absurd employment
they ended regretting their prowess,
years I have seen dozing on my father's chest
businessman, farmer, wine-distiller
& on my mother, primary teacher, or my relatives

after the loss of their last orchards,
one was from the mountains & the warm valleys,
now they sit on their doorsteps & listen to gossip
hoping their children get their own little house
with a garden & sun, & avoid suffering.
Years that flap in the wind
like canvas tents on the abandoned beaches
of an indigo Lima; so many old men
with beautiful manners, waiting for time to end
with a certain timidity & sweetness that proclaims
their innocent journey through wealth;
these are the old bourgoisie
in a world more conformist than all the lost worlds
because the new ones grow with foreign aid or dictatorships
& today they sponsor politicians or anti-cancer foundations.
But it's sure that both are guilty
because man is guilty of having been born into his environment
without even a conscience, only the hate that embellishes it
with these new sufferings.
        And after the 'thirties
the excited boys drinking quickly searched the streets
in groups for the single face that haunted them.
Foolish & beautiful deaths
all night in the fields
running from dogs & shots, or in the jails
sick, listening to slangy conversations on Quijote
& the coming social justice.
Afterwards nearly all, quiet & drawn,
buried their youth.
Hard laws of conversation
bloodless alliances & the plans of the government,
& enthusiastic crowds down the length of the road
bright with paper & flowers

in the afternoon sun.
And the young men of the 'forties & 'fifties
still turn in these same sails
of the windmill yellow with the quick straws of time,
swollen with strength & brilliance
the waters reverberate
but again the streets empty
& it doesn't move a single stone of my country.
Boys of the 'fifties in the schoolrooms & books
European literature & the specialisation,
you could also be repressed,
growing old & unknown
& some idiot will call you founders.
And then there's us too
persecuted by old words,
we dispute new rivers,
& the woods slide against the castle
in the greater rebellion, that of dying,
guerrillas in Junín or Cuzco
weighted our shadows with rumour
but nobody will gossip again
like magpies in the hour of slaughter
because the lament is not equal to the despair.
Today I have all my strength
the time rides out in passion
for the time that has not yet ceased;
boys that do not feel this
like grapes in a wicker sun
because of the pain don't ask me
'come on, let's walk
through the streets again
in search of the quick gold
that we love in the face that haunts us

in the depths of our flesh & this land.'
I sing here of youth
& you who will move the stones.

Translated by Ena Hollis

Mirko Lauer

The Angels

What the devil are these angels doing perched half-way between
    heaven & earth?
They're lodged on several worm-eaten cornices of wood
    motionless above the sky of Lima;
& on the road from Callao there's a figure-head, a chunk of
    heaven that has nothing to do with us but *in caelum*
& on the corner of Camaná & Quilca there's a worn-out
    plaster cherubim
with an excessively angelic look
        obstinately hooked into the air by its long finger-nails:
aurum et argentum. What do we look like to them?
        What do they think of our troubles & problems?
They never move,
never descend from the outer world, from their domains,
        yet in the obstinate darkness of their corners
have something to say to all of us
by their very presence in the air like an unattainable point of
    reference.
        The angels
are all plaster—someone has to say it—all wooden,
well-polished & varnished, totally unlike our bones
        & one has a trumpet, another a sword
but none a heart of flesh or a job six days a week.
No doubt their bugles blow day & night
        & are suspended in the air of our thoughts,
their swords always ready
judging the sense of human action. In this same city

there's a cupola full of angels talking of things of another century.
all golden & hard, made from ancient wood,
stone angels totally impassive,
sane & asexual, leaving or entering the gate between their two worlds.
They giggle & chat, display their little breasts
ex comodo, in spiritualibus
cathedrals of self-sufficient light precariously perched
above a land that doesn't belong to them.

Translated by David Tipton

Cruel Photograph without Light at Daybreak

N.N.
seated on a stool, in a bar, without companions,
face furrowed by a trickle of silver-nitrate, all the sadness
in his smile that shows the years of drinking, a frayed sleeve,
60 years in Lima, his soul tired & ugly,
exactly like its own expressions,
& the monstrous gods he can't banish through alcohol
smiling at him & the little god, Ganymedes, running from his call,
the truth revealed in this dark bar by its confusion,
& the fates not daring to beckon him
wait for a bad moment,
& he
surprised in his squalid revelry, without lights or patronage,
a prisoner, with his baggy eyelids, caught this side the grave
in the darkness of shadows with the poor consolation of being
St. John the Blasphemer,
at the moment when repentence is frustrated

by the gay arrival of the strippers
& optimism returns.
But it's the time when night yields & salvation hasn't come,
& he
blind, deaf, dumb, crippled, maimed & intellectual
sounding out his image mirrored a 1000 times in the blue-print
of his veins
fixes his gaze
& they come
the acids that can eat away a body & undermine a look
sulphur-coloured, capable of tattoing an insect between the eyes,
that simmer in the minds of the old while they doze,
& the hearts of delicate old men already sleeping,
the acids that whirl,
sprinkling a table of goodbyes,
& days spent
between the greetings of beautiful women & agile boys
who jump up & escape.
And rebellion crumples, shuts its eyes, hides its face
& from the marble tables that illumine a life a light's turned off,
at such times a man is racked by a cruel circus of eyes.
And the gods don't give a damn for their old rival.

Translated by David Tipton

The Classics Revisited

I fought that war
& lost in it
fortune & woman: nine years
bearing banners/images

& other gadgets of the gods.
Nine years
breathing life
into the wooden animals
& that ninth year
almost driving us crazy
begging each other for cigarettes & matches
'God damn that woman'
& she
keeping till the end of the war
her body in apparent shape
primadona
with her aquiline profile & buttocks
like those of an old mare
fit
for the dreams of a soldier
& for pornographic photographs.
Young woman,
we had to fight for her,
& when at last we entered,
they say
we couldn't recognize her
pale
prosperity of the kingdom
her youth lost in the markets
she was worn out & sad
in the autumn of her days, sipping tea
in the interior gardens.

Translated by David Tipton

Tanks

Co ye to?
Crossing the frontier
the soviet tanks took us
cold that Holy Saturday.
Two years ago
no one had a thing against them
this year
the echoes from across the border
resounded to the hills.
The Srtas. Ortiz
were leaving the Odeon cinema.
The public
preferred the blonde one,
& an angry old man
whistled at the screen indignantly.
The news was a year old then
but our tanks
have been here for many springs.
In winter
they take them on manoevres in Sacsahuamán.
In summer
protect their toad-like bellies
beneath green awnings.
What're they guarding?
The frontiers
are distant
& only the lone old man
whistles at the screen.

Translated by David Tipton

STATEMENTS & COMMENT

On the Situation of the Writer in Peru

Antonio Cisneros

My country is under-developed, without definite cultural forms of its own, facing towards the North to which it gives discreet approval and is ever ready to imitate. Peru has a fabulous past, but that 'past' doesn't belong to me, and I can only appreciate its remains like any foreigner. I know we're distinct, but how? That's the question.

The consciousness of being under-developed is growing and also the strength necessary to terminate this situation. Cuba has shown to the West the new face of Latin-America, and to the countries which are the Spanish versions of the northern masters, a way, that before we only knew about from books and proclamations. In a few years the West may be able to call us *wild* and *passionate* but not *picturesque*.

Vallejo, I think, has given a pre-eminence to poetry here, a prestige and security for the writer just beginning that, real or false, beginners in the other arts don't have. Yet it's not the poetry itself that dominates my generation but the possibility of establishing the validity of Peruvian poetry in an international context which Vallejo has given us. This prestige means that in a country almost without publishers a disproportionate amount of poetry—good, fair, bad and terrible—is printed. Four out of five anthologies are devoted to it; it abounds in the few literary magazines, and cultural occasions have their basis in a poetry recital. To get certain jobs a couple of books of published verse can help. I'm not saying the poet is applauded by those in power, or that he can live comfortably in society, but that in the small cultural world of Lima he can flutter around with a certain elegance almost never well-deserved.

What can I say about the poetry itself? We've always been influenced by poetry others have created in distant countries. In a sense we're translators. Fashions come and go, and all leave some trace. Surrealism fed our poets for nearly two generations but is no longer much of an influence; perhaps an interest in English poetry has grown (three weeks ago a friend of mine discovered T. S. Eliot). But it doesn't seem to me that we read more or less than before—perhaps a little more widely in other languages as you find more translations around. Conflicts between 'Social', 'Pure' and 'Elitist' groups have become of far less importance and the dispute between Academics and Non-academics appears to have been buried. Whatever happens, as I've said, fashions come and go, though I don't think this generation differs essentially. The actual work of a writer is the same as it's always been: to be a witness of reality, no matter which aspect of it he chooses.

Rodolfo Hinostroza

1960. The University of San Marcos. It appears I accused some young poets of mixing a little Lorca, a little Neruda and a little Vallejo to make their social poetry. . . . César Calvo's popularity seemed to me facile; the emulation of Naranjo and Corcuera parochial. Among my friends I talked of 'working in darkness'. I rediscovered Joyce and Perse. I study the former exhaustively. San Marcos accused me of being idle or vicious: that's the writer's situation. At the best of times we're suspect. Our hearts are to the Left, in some cases our whole body, with others, the head only. I read *Portrait of an Artist.* Adolescence: the turbulent loves and long letter-poems of an experimental sort, bui the projected *Song to Cuba* in the style of Perse was never written. And after the polemics with the *Social-realists* suspicious of rebellion, and the absurd quarrel with the *Pure* poets, I chose a third position: of negativity. Javier Heraud found at the bottom of polemics only empty words; he denied the word and died in action. The flag-wavers, the scoffers and accusers among the *Social-realists* give nothing, but run, cry out, then prudently shut up. Something of value from that period? Perhaps Romualdo's high-flown *Túpac Amaru*, or Rose's *Song to Walt Whitman*.

Anyway no one knows anything; no one has a system of aesthetics. There's the school of Rose, of Romualdo, of Sologuren and of Delgado. I go around with *Ulysses* under my arm. Has anyone read *Ulysses*? 'Yes, some parts.' 'Yes, vaguely.' 'Joyce was a reactionary Jesuit.' I read aloud some lines of Perse. A young poet interrupts me and says that Perse was a conformist who praised the established order. A reactionary!

There's a house near the Baths of Barranco called 'The House of Poetry'. and Romualdo's disciples want to call it, 'The Tower of the Hallucinated', but nobody reads Lautreamont or Rimbaud or Michaux. The name is charming, that's all. There're people who write:

I love a certain shadow and a certain light
that mingled together, give I believe
a certain blueness to the profound houses of the dead.

That's Eielson. Good poetry? And Eielson? They say he went to Europe. He, and Westphalen are the best of the Surrealists. And Martín Adán, commendable and slandered. Then we find there's another frantic anti-Limean appearing in some Surrealist anthologies, César Moro, who wrote in French. That is our literary tradition. Those our schools. Vallejo's neither a writer nor a man, but a myth. One can't say, '*Los Heraldos Negros* is not enough'. Or, 'he didn't *have* to die of hunger'. That's totem and tabu. Neither do we have anything to do, either in time or space, with the Spanish Civil War, but we get enthusiastic about its little songs and million dead:

Though they blow the bridge and the gang-plank
they'll see us cross the Ebro in a little boat.

One's supposed to say Miguel Hernández was a great poet, and what a pity about Lorca, and the fat Guillén, and Pablo Neruda, what a pity he was a diplomatist. Things and voices that say nothing to us now, that belong to other consciences. Ours is different, we say. But what's different? Isn't it true we have revolutionary ideals? Aren't we confirmed Marxists? Isn't it true we write for the people?

To the wall, to the wall with suffering
to the wall with the father of the lamb . . .
to the wall with my own poetry
if it doesn't sing of the things it ought . . ,

recited Rose. Ovation in the Hall of San Marcos. And the social poets grew on the shoulders of the Party, on the shoulders of the Cuban Revolution. But time passed; they killed Heraud, the guerrillas were destroyed, and poets had to submit to being judged by their written work. An enormous shipwreck. The shoulders of the Party are worth nothing when mediocre poets lean upon them. It's useless being an official poet when literary history concerns itself only with the actual work. They never tried to emulate Dante, but only Hernández, an uncultured patriotic man who sang in the trenches. And from this nothing has survived. 'The age demanded . . .' But did they know what was demanded of our time? Had they studied, with lucidity and passion, and without prejudice, what the age demanded? Did they want to stop history in 1936? A wonderful confusion continues. Someone, sometime will write, *Portrait of the Artist as a young Latin-American.* And it's true many people felt guilty about writing after Heraud's death, and no longer spoke at all of an interest in poetic technique. So we've inherited a confusion that comes down from our Colonial Period, and which the various groups today still project. Critics like vultures feed on the corpses and say the same things about mediocre as they do about comparatively good work, discrediting themselves morally and professionally. They're only harsh with obviously atrocious work no one would dare defend.

The function of the writer: suspicion. His situation: a certain ambiguity. His is essentially a defensive attitude. One of anger and impotence. Who reads us and who publishes us? How much does each poet lose on his book? I lost something like 6000 *soles* (£60); which is to say, I pay the public to read me. They then accuse me of being 'hermetic' or something. Of writing unpopular poetry. Do you find my words obscure? The obscurity is in your souls.

We mustn't deceive ourselves; our readers are of the *Reader's Digest* level and we only succeed if we write with no technical innovations and no rigour. Poetry must be clean and transparent like water, and written from inspiration according to the best romantic tradition. 1964. Havana. I published *The Night* in the magazine of Casa de las Americas. Agitation! It ought to have been obvious. I should have known. They accuse me of immorality. Not a question of defending oneself. Men of good will are being used to delay the advance of culture.

'A nude Greek is very different to a nude Peruvian,' it's said. If for example I lean on the Puente de Piedra gazing at the Rio Rimac and meditate about 'Time' and 'Heraclitus' and *vanitas vanitatum*, I'm a naked Peruvian, but if T. S. Eliot gazes at the Thames flowing and meditates too, he's a nude Greek. And it's not a question of comparing quality but of the reactions of the reader to those writers who dare speak of 'universal things'. I suppose confronted by this situation there're people who flee their country—Eliot, Joyce, Pound, or that exile themselves in an imaginary never-

never land like Borges and Lezama Lima. It's understandable.

Who used to say the inexpressible doesn't exist? It wasn't Byron. Flaubert coined the phrase which Joyce picked up and made into a creed through which he tried to perfect his means of expression to include a far greater range of reality and experience in his work. Those men were literary monks in fact with a passion for work beyond the ordinary. It's not enough to suffer like Vallejo to write like him. And it's not enough to receive the praise of critics. In truth nothing can be enough. Midas told us a story fit for children or idiots, and the only worthwhile advice is: work, work incessantly. 'The rest is dross,' as Pound said.

On the Death of Javier Heraud

Washington Delgado, Lima 24th May, 1963

Everyone connected in some way with Javier Heraud has been deeply moved by his death. It's something more than a sad anecdote; it illumines the dark times in which we live. So let's think for a moment on the meaning of his short life; search for the essence of his tragedy. For we cannot give him better homage.

A lot has already been said and written about the events of Puerto Maldonado. They've been described as romantic adventure, heroic, useless or stupid. But all of these qualifications are purely emotional and only serve to illustrate the attitudes of the commentators. No one has tried to explain these events logically and coherently, yet they don't conceal any mystery or complexity but are on the contrary open and transparent.

Revolution, it is said, stems from dream or madness. And revolution in Peru must be carefully planned and organised with caution; so that it's necessary to wait for the right occasion and favourable conditions; and that while waiting for these to emerge the revolutionary should perfect himself; study, read, think, write and conspire in secret. Is this true? I'm not discussing the necessity for the revolution. Heraud and his companions didn't discuss this problem either. They had already discussed it, in every aspect, and were decided upon action. I'm not analysing the validity of revolution, but merely, shall we say, its mechanics. I don't believe the revolutionary studies or plans for anything else but revolution. He doesn't wait for conditions but makes history. For revolution only comes about when men act in a revolutionary manner. From this point of view the events of Puerto Maldonado are both logical and coherent.

It's necessary to refute another objection to the procedure adopted by Heraud. Its violence. Many people think that violence is inhuman and irrational, and they're right. Im not a thinker, nor a philosopher, I'm not a revolutionary, but I like to talk clearly and not delude myself with fallacies. I'm a sceptical bourgeois, an epicurean and an egotist; and if Heraud had consulted me before going to die I would probably havc tried to dissuade him. Now no one can discourage him. He's dead and I'm alive, and it's shameful to repeat the nonsense that has been said, or to retreat behind an ambiguous statement. There's a truth that arises from Heraud's death and one shouldn't keep silent about it. He was my friend and I know he was good from his finger-tips to the bottom of his soul; and whoever else knew him could testify the same. I know he was intelligent and lucid; whoever has read his verses would say the same. Such a man may be mistaken, but cannot act irrationally. For if revolution means barbarous and irrational violence, Heraud accepted it. Revolution doesn't create violence; it already exists in the world. Read whatever history book you like and you end up with an image of ferocity and bloodshed. For horror and brutality no story by Poe, Kafka or Dashiel Hammett can exceed the crime pages of the daily newspapers in Lima. Go out into the street, look at the beggars in the centre of the city and the prostitutes in the poor suburbs, walk through the Red Light district, enter its infamous bars. Easy to grant that those who live and work there have to degrade themselves in order to survive. Would they live in that way unless a blind force, a cold and methodical violence did not oppress them? Not to mention the peasants on the land; the families thrown out of huts they built with their own hands. Revolution in any case claims to be the final act of violence; the remedy to a violent society.

Is revolution the only way to end this misery? I don't know. I'd like to say, no, there're other bloodless ways, but I'm not sure. Whatever the case Heraud answered in the affirmative and died because that answer was honorable. We may think he was mistaken but we can't say he acted like a child or that he was deceived, His death is a lesson in moral integrity, in humanity. Right or wrong his conduct was honest.

I've tried to explain the events of Puerto Maldonado, but a last question remains: is it just that Heraud died? That a writer capable perhaps of some great works should perish? What did he die for? What was the purpose of his life? One may ask: why and for what do all of us have to live? And above all how much time do we have? A month, a year, perhaps ten or fifty. Who knows for certain? Perhaps something will survive us; a bridge, a house, a garden, some poems. But they'll also disappear. So will the town and country in which we live. The earth upon which we tread will perish too. And with it, or after it, the sun itself. Such is the physical law of the universe. Yet we elevate the miniscule world of humanity whose laws seem to be: propagation and progress.

It's sad to die through accident or disease. Seward, the Duke of Northumberland, sick in his bed, feeling the approach of death, is alleged to have said: 'What shame to have survived so many wars, only to finish this way, like a cow.' 'I want to die my own death not that of the doctors,' Rilke exclaimed, trapped by gangrene. We possess nothing so intimately as death and it's beautiful to have a singular and personal one such as that which contributes to and serves humanity; the death of the mother for her child or the death of a man for his country.

Javier Heraud had the courage to choose his death, and the privilege of dying in a manner neither banal nor egotistical. Time will pass and a day will come when no one will remember his name. But he died for us, his friends and enemies, for the poor and for the rich, for the masters and the slaves. He died in the end for a history no one can stop.

Autobiographical Comment

Sebastián Salazar Bondy

I was born in Calle Corazón de Jesús, in Chacarilla near the Church of the Orphans, the heart of Lima. My home was typical of the middle-class, formed by old property-owning families from the provinces impoverished by the imperialist invasion and the life of luxury and pomp the aristocracy brought from their native lands. I was descended from French immigrants and a Jewish family from the ghettoes of Prague. My father came from the north, Chiclayo, and established in Lima a relatively good social and economic position through business which underwent a crisis that led to its break-up, and his death in 1933.

My childhood, intimately shared with Augusto, my brother, was, I think, deeply affected by that economic crisis which meant the loss of our car and certain luxuries, such as the promise of an education in Europe; and a strict economy—our house was converted into a pensión for gentlemen, preferably foreigners, to help solve the financial problem. From then on I saw the world divided into irreconcilable halves.

My father, who had taken part in politics as a partisan of

General Sánchez Cerro, had been surrounded by powerful and important friends. He was gone, and those friendships which meant expensive presents at Christmas time disappeared too. Before the crisis I was studying at the German College, but this also changed; we had to go to San Augustín College in Lima, a typical middle-class school then, where I became acquainted with the world of religion, and at the same time of repression, inhibition, prohibition, prejudice and humiliation—'Salazar, tell your brother that he owes two months' fees and that if he doesn't pay you can't take the examination.'

Around my eleventh year I first discovered the need to express myself through writing which I did so secretly my teachers never found out. This necessity for literary expression accompanied by a precocious and chaotic reading had both a positive and negative result. The positive thing was that I reached a stage of development others usually reach much later. The negative that I prematurely published pages which shame me now, reappearing in bookshops like ghosts to haunt me.

I wrote poetry, drama and fiction because I had an intuition confirmed later by certain theories that the branches of literature were not separate institutions, but instruments one employed according to what one wanted to say. Literature then was a mode of expression not limited to a single road. I had luck too. There was the friendship of two writers, Javier Sologuren and Jorge Eielson, whose conversation enriched me enormously. To them I voiced my ideas, and through them affirmed the seriousness of my vocation. There were also painters such as Fernando de Szyszlo, older writers among the best in Peru, José María Arguedas and Westphalen; my professor at San Marcos, Fabio Xammar; Manuel Moreno Jimeno and many others. To all of them I owe a little of what has worth in my work.

I'm not particularly a short-story writer but I've written some stories into which I've put something that interested me: the small mythology of the middle-class world; the subtlety of its relationships sewn and tacked together by prejudices and deep feelings, inherited ideas accepted irrationally and aspirations that are never achieved, frustrated hopes and terrors. I think I've captured the situation of tension that exists among the middle-class everywhere, but especially in an under-developed country where the only people who live authentic lives are the rich through possession of the economic means, the instruments of power and all the insolence that this gives; and the working-class who live resigned to their misery, accepting it and converting it into a strength; yes their poverty is one of their strengths. Those who live inauthentic lives are those that social and economic reality pulls down, while their dreams push them up. They're in an intermediate position in which any negligence can drag them down to the working-class and certain kinds of treachery carry them towards the prosperity of the rich. This is the world I've described for it's the one I know and live in, and believe moreover is socially important despite its precarious position, for from it come the intellectuals, the teachers and leaders of revolution. It's the class that consolidates the culture of the country and thus holds its conscience. In its tenacious struggle for life it daily threatens the rich by its impetus and aspirations that sometimes destroy even the racial barriers so furious among such people.

It was during the first journey I made to Buenos Aires where I lived for some years that I discovered Peru, not the Peru of the hymns and symbols, but the reality. It was there I found statistics telling me Peru was one of the hungriest nations in the world, with one of the highest infant-mortality rates; one of the most exploited or semi-colonised in Latin America; one of the saddest. But there too I found I couldn't live without it and if I had some duty compatible with my work as a writer, it was to expose those conditions and to use my words, in as much as they had influence, to free it. That's why I'm a socialist, for I think that the capitalist society, above all when capitalism is inserted into a marginal world—source of raw materials and under-paid labour—morally defeats a country. One cannot talk of national defence granted that the fundamental strength of a country, its moral strength and consciousness of its sovereignty, is subjugated. It was then I began to believe in Peru, its people and history, and stopped believing at the same time in the symbols and grand words, the ephemera that accumulates through legend and myth.

The four prose documents are translated by David Tipton

BIOGRAPHICAL NOTES

SEBASTIAN SALAZAR BONDY, born in Lima 1924 and died in 1965, published several selections of poetry, short stories and criticism. Perhaps his best-known book is *Lima la Horrible*, 1964, a bitter indictment of the city. All the poems in this anthology are from his last volume, *El Tacto de la Araña*, published posthumously in 1966.

FRANCISCO CARRILLO, born in 1925, has published several books of poetry and edited many anthologies of poems and short stories. He also edits and publishes the influential poetry magazine *Haraui*. The translations here are from his collected poems *En Busca del Tema Poético*, 1965. He has just published a novel, *Unas Vacaciones Perdidas*.

WASHINGTON DELGADO, born in Cuzco in 1927, has published four volumes of poetry, the first, *Formas de la Ausencia* in 1955, the last, *Parque*, 1965. He won the National Poetry Prize in 1953, and co-edits the magazine, *Visión del Perú*. The poems here are from his recent uncollected work.

CARLOS GERMAN BELLI, born in 1928, is at present in Europe on a Guggenheim awarded for his poetry. He spent a session teaching at the Iowa Writers' Workshop in 1969. He has published five volumes of poetry including, *O Hada Cibernética*, 1961, from which most of these translations are taken, and *El Pie sobre el cuello*, 1964.

PABLO GUEVARA, born in Lima in 1930, has published three books of poetry, the most important of which is *Los Habitantes*, 1965, from which five of the poems here are taken. He has lived for some years in Europe, but is now living on a small farm near Lima.

RODOLFO HINOSTROZA, born in Lima in 1941, but spent part of his childhood in Huaráz. He has lived in Cuba and at the moment is living in Paris. His only published book, *Consejero del Lobo*, appeared in 1965. A recent collection, *Muerte de York*, should be out soon in Mexico.

ANTONIO CISNEROS, born in Lima, 1942, has published four books, including *Comentarios Reales*, which won the national poetry prize in

1965, and *Canto ceremonial contra un oso hormiguero*, published by Casa de las Americas, Havana, in 1968, and which won their prize for the whole of Latin America. A selection of his poetry in English translation is being published by Cape-Goliard, 1970. Cisneros has lived and taught in England, and at the moment is lecturing at Nice, France.

JAVIER HERAUD was born in 1942 and killed by the police in Puerto Maldonado, a remote town in the eastern jungle in 1963. His collected poems were published in 1964 under the title, *javier heraud / poesías completas y homenaje*.

MARCOS MARTOS, born in Piura in 1942, and at present teaching at the University of Ayachucho, has published one book of poetry, *Casa Nuestra*, from which the poems here are taken. He has also represented Peru at chess.

JULIO ORTEGA, born in Chimbote in 1942, has published three books of poetry, his most recent, *las viñas de moro*, 1968. He has also published short stories, plays and criticism. At the moment he is lecturing on Spanish Literature at Pennsylvania in the USA.

MIRKO LAUER, born in 1947, of Czechoslovakian descent, and educated in Lima and Canada, has published two books, the last *Ciudad de Lima*, 1968. He is working with the government at the moment, and has another volume ready to publish.